A Gu

Insight Meditation

Attaining Nibbāna
with the Earliest Buddhist Teachings
using Mindfulness of Lovingkindness

Bhante Vimalaraṁsi

with David Johnson

Publisher: Dhamma Sukha Publishing
ISBN-10: 1508569711
ISBN-13: 978-1508569718
Published: 1ˢᵗ Edition July 2015
2ⁿᵈ Edition: July 2017

Other books by Bhante Vimalaraṁsi:

The Dhamma Leaf Series, 2014
Meditation is Life, Life is Meditation, 2014
Moving Dhamma Volume 1, 2012
Breath of Love, 2011

Other books by David Johnson:

The Path to Nibbāna, 2017 (the follow-on book to this book with advanced practice and instructions)

For those who wish to experience

the Cessation of Suffering

through the Elimination of Craving

Contents

Introduction

The purpose of this guide is to help someone who is new to meditation, and the Buddha's teachings walk the Buddha's path to the destruction of Craving and the elimination of Ignorance. This guide will provide you with the basic meditation instructions for the practice of Tranquil Wisdom Insight Meditation (TWIM) as taught by Bhante Vimalaraṁsi. TWIM is the actual Brahmavihāras practice described in the suttas, and it includes the Divine Dwellings of Mindfulness of Lovingkindness (*Mettā*), Mindfulness of Compassion (*Karuṇā*), Mindfulness of Joy (*Muditā*), and Mindfulness of Equanimity (*Upekkhā*).

The Brahmavihāras are described by the Buddha in his earliest talks as recorded in the suttas of the Majjhima Nikāya[1]. The instructions in this guide are based on the suttas themselves and on commentaries that are consistent with the suttas. The instructions explain Right Effort — this is what we call the "6Rs". The 6Rs will be explained in detail later.

Most Buddhist Mindfulness practices today tend to focus on the breath as the object of meditation. They only use Mettā and the Brahmavihāras as "side meditations" to help one with relaxation and as a way of "softening" the breath practice and of softening life in general.

However, the Buddha discussed the Mindfulness of Mettā practice many more times in the suttas than the Mindfulness of Breathing (*Ānāpānasati*) practice: only eight times for Mindfulness of Breathing and more than a hundred times for the Mindfulness of Lovingkindness.

Although many teachers today do not teach this or support this view, the Buddha *did* state that the Mettā and Brahmavihāras

---

1   *The Middle Length Discourses of the Buddha*, trans. Bhikkhu Bodhi and Bhikkhu Ñāṇamoli (Somerville, MA: Wisdom Publications, 1995).

practice, on its own, will lead to the supreme attainment of Nibbāna. The sutta *Accompanied by Lovingkindness* in the Saṃyutta Nikāya (46:54(4)) makes this clear.[2]

Tranquil Wisdom Insight Meditation, using Mettā or the feeling of Lovingkindness as the object of meditation, has been found to be easier and to give faster results than using the Breath as the object of meditation. It includes a powerful warm and *glowing* feeling, which helps your practice because you enjoy doing it. When practicing this meditation, you are radiating Lovingkindness, and giving this feeling to others. This is building your generosity while simultaneously developing a greater sense of well-being and contentment. You are doing this not only while engaged in your formal sitting practice but also throughout your daily life experience. This creates momentum from the time you get up in the morning until the time you go to sleep. This continuous practice can be very conducive to fast progress.

TWIM includes an all-important step that is found in the suttas but is misunderstood or left out of most Buddhist Mindfulness practices these days. This step is the key to the attainment of Nibbāna! You will learn more about this later; this is the *Relax Step.*

This book is a guide to beginning practice. A deeper understanding of how TWIM works, descriptions of insights, levels of understanding that arise, and the sutta references that support this meditation are all beyond the scope of this booklet. The book *Meditation is Life; Life is Meditation*[3] provides that information in depth and detail. Other books like *Breath of Love*[4] and *Moving Dhamma*[5] also offer skillful guidance once you are deeper in the

---

2   See also our website www.dhammasukha.org for more discussion on this subject.
3   Bhante Vimalaraṁsi, *Meditation is Life, Life is Meditation* (Annapolis: Dhamma Sukha Publishing, 2014).
4   Vimalaraṁsi, Breath of Love (Jakarta, Indonesia: Ehipassiko Publishing)

practice. A book by senior student Doug Kraft, *Buddha's Map*[6], is another good reference for the concepts and experiences of TWIM.

5   Vimalaraṁsi, *Moving Dhamma*, vol. 1 (Annapolis, MO: Dhamma Sukha Publishing, 2012). Vimalaraṁsi, Breath of Love (Jakarta, Indonesia: Ehipassiko Publishing)

6   Doug Kraft, *Buddha's Map* (Grass Valley, CA: Blue Dolphin Publishing, 2013).

What is Mindfulness?

The term "Mindfulness" has become commonplace these days and is often interpreted differently than what I believe was originally formulated by the Buddha.

You may have heard that Mindfulness is watching what arises, diving into it, and focusing firmly on it to understand the nature of what arises. The idea is that concentrating more closely and harder on the "object of meditation," will ultimately yield profound insights.

However, that is not the Mindfulness that the Buddha taught; rather, that is called one-pointed concentration: absorbing your attention into an object.

The Buddha learned from his experiences and described in sutta 36 of the Majjhima Nikāya, the Mahāsaccaka Sutta, that one-pointed concentration will quiet the mind temporarily, but it will not lead to an understanding of suffering and the cause of suffering, or to Nibbāna. For that reason, the Buddha rejected absorption and one-pointed concentration practices. Most teachers today miss this significant point. Yet sutta 36 does spell it out. The Buddha rejected the teachings of Ālāra Kalama and Uddaka Rāmaputta—teachers of the most advanced concentration states of the time. He left their training to continue his search for yet another six years.

Here is a short, clear, and precise definition of Mindfulness as the Buddha taught it:

Mindfulness means to remember to observe
how mind's attention moves
from one thing to another.

The first part of Mindfulness is to *remember* to watch the mind and remember to return to your object of meditation when you

4

have wandered off. The second part of Mindfulness is to *observe* how mind's attention moves from one thing to another.

Real insight is gained by watching how your mind interacts with things, as they arise—not by observing the things themselves. True mindfulness is *remembering* to *observe* how your mind moves and responds to what arises in the present moment.

With mindfulness, we can understand how things arise and pass away, from beginning to end. We do not care *why* things arise—that is the concern of psychologists and philosophers. We only care about *how* they arise and *how* they pass away—how the movement of mind's attention happens during that entire process.

When mindfulness becomes strong, you start to understand what Craving really is. Craving is what pulls your mind away from your object of meditation. Tensions and tightness arise with sensations and thoughts. Craving is what starts the identification process in which you take something personally with an "I like it" or "I don't like it" mind.

Mindfulness meditation is the process of observing how mind's attention moves moment-to-moment. Mindfulness enables us to see clearly and precisely *how* the impersonal process of thoughts and sensations arises and passes away.[7] We identify with this process as ourselves; we take it personally. Seeing and understanding how mind's attention moves from one thing to another, personalizing experience and creating an "I" as it goes, is one of the most important insights of this practice. It develops an impersonal perspective on all arising phenomena and leads the meditator to see for themselves the true nature of existence. You finally answer the question, "Who (or what) am I?"

The other important facet of mindfulness, once we have remembered and observed, is to catch ourselves when we get lost—

---

7   The Buddha called this process Dependent Origination or Paṭiccasamuppāda.

to remember that we are supposed to "come back home." More on this as we explain the 6R process later.

Why do we practice Mettā?

As was said earlier, the Buddha talked about Mettā meditation far more frequently than he talked about Breath Meditation, and he made clear that Mettā meditation, as part of the Brahmavihāras, will lead to Nibbāna. Those are good enough reasons in and of themselves to incline us toward Mettā meditation. Nevertheless, there are other reasons as well.

First, using the suttas as the guide, Dhamma Sukha teaches Mindfulness of Breath (Ānāpānasati) differently than other techniques which are one-pointed. Breath practice that focuses and concentrates on the nose tip or belly is not found in the suttas. The Buddha never said to concentrate on the breath — he said to observe and to know what the breath is doing in the moment and to observe what mind's attention was doing as we are breathing. As the mind starts to wander away, this is where we employ the 6Rs, to softly, without any pushing away, bring back our observation to the object of meditation.[8]

We would prefer that those meditators who have practiced Breath Meditation in the past use a completely different object of meditation. Otherwise, they may habitually revert to the way they were taught, using what we very much consider "bad habits." This can lead to confusion and a lack of progress. We prefer to avoid a practice that requires people to struggle against their old ways of practicing.

Second, we find that Mindfulness of Mettā and the practice of the Brahmavihāras is easier because of the comfortable feeling of Mettā. This is especially important for the beginner, because Breath Meditation may be difficult to master since it is more of a mental

---

8 For more information on how the Breath Meditation is taught by us, please check our website, www.dhammasukha.org, for a talk on the Satipaṭṭhāna Sutta in which we go through a complete explanation.

exercise. With Mindfulness of Mettā, because of its pleasant nature, you can also stay with your object longer, and it is more fun to do. It's probably strange hearing that meditation can be fun!

Third, we have seen in actual practice that progress is much faster with Mettā *because* the feeling of Mettā itself is quite pleasant. Remember that this is a *feeling* meditation, and it is a *pleasant*, happy feeling.

Finally, Mettā meditation, again being a *feeling* meditation, distances you from any other "body"-based or sensation types of meditation which involve concentrating on parts of your body. It focuses on a feeling of loving-kindness. It avoids any "bad habits" that you might have picked up.

So, let's get started!

Beginning Posture

Before meditating, it is helpful to find a relatively quiet place and to sit comfortably and upright.

Sitting cross-legged is not required, the full lotus is certainly not necessary. A sitting posture that is familiar to your body will be less distracting and more helpful than one in which you are uncomfortable or in pain. In the West, many meditators find sitting on the floor difficult. In that case, use a chair rather than causing yourself undue pain and discomfort. There is no "magic" in the floor.

Avoid leaning heavily back into the chair. Sit with your vertebrae stacked one on top of the other. The posture should be comfortable. The goals are to reduce any real physical cause of tension and pain and to improve alertness. We will have enough *mental* obstacles to keep us busy!

Beginning Lovingkindness Instructions

When you practice the *Mindfulness of Lovingkindness* meditation, begin by radiating loving and kind feelings to yourself. Remember a time when you were happy. When that happy feeling arises, it is a warm, glowing feeling.

Some of you may complain—we actually do hear this a lot—that you cannot recall any good memories. So, then we ask, "Can you imagine holding a baby and looking into its eyes? Do you feel a loving feeling? When that baby smiles, do *you*?"

Another idea is to imagine holding a cute little puppy. When you look at the puppy, you naturally want to smile and play with him. The feeling you are creating is a warm, glowing, and sincere feeling radiating from your eyes, your mind, and your heart.

Once you have established this feeling, use this feeling to wish yourself happiness. "Just as I was happy then, may I be happy now." Continue with phrases like "May I be peaceful," "May I be happy," "May I be calm."

Do you know what it feels like to be peaceful and calm? Then *put that feeling* and *yourself* in the center of your heart and surround yourself with that happy feeling.

When that feeling fades, bring up another phrase to remind you of the feeling. "May I be tranquil," "May I be content," "May I be full of joy." Now give yourself a big "heart hug." Really and sincerely, wish yourself to be happy! Love yourself and mean it. This feeling is your object of meditation.

Each time the feeling fades, repeat the wish verbally a few times in your mind. Just repeat it enough times to bring up the feeling—*do not* make it a mantra! Saying a phrase over and over will not bring up the feeling we want — the phrase just reminds us to bring the feeling up. When the feeling comes up we drop the phrase.

There are a number of other teachers who focus on just saying the phrases over and over, and that doesn't work. That will just turn it into a concentration practice on the phrase.

Some people visualize easily; others do not. It is not important that you clearly *see* your object of meditation. Just *know* it is there. Keep the feeling of yourself in the center of your chest, wrapped in this happy and content feeling.

And, we do mean really *feel good!* Feel peaceful, or calm, or loving, or gentle, or kind, or giving, or joyful, or clear, or tranquil, or accepting. Be okay sitting and feeling this. It's *okay* to feel good, let yourself be there in the present, just feeling this contentment.

You have nowhere to go; you are on a little vacation from life now. There is nothing to do other than to be happy and radiate that feeling to yourself. Can you do that? Don't *try* to be happy. *Be* happy! Be content. Be at peace—right here, right now. You have our permission to be happy for at least the next thirty minutes!

This is a feeling meditation, but don't over observe the center of your chest trying to bring up a feeling of Lovingkindness. Don't force a feeling where there isn't one. Don't put the cart before the horse. Smile and feel that smile all through your body. As you say the phrases, bring this feeling up, and it will resonate in your heart area on its own. *Sincerely* wish yourself happiness. Believe it, and know that you *do* wish happiness for yourself. Just be with this feeling, know it is there, and smile with it.

There may be some blocks that come up such as saying to yourself, "No, I don't deserve to be happy like this!" This aversion to your own happiness is a distraction. Distractions will be covered shortly. We will explain the method to deal with them so that you can allow and train yourself to feel real Lovingkindness for a longer period of time.

Later, when you begin feeling this feeling toward others, know that similar blocks may come up and that these are distractions too.

There is no reason that others should not be happy as well. The goal is first to accept and allow yourself to be happy and peaceful. It's okay. Then, since you feel that happiness in your own mind you will be happy to share that feeling with other beings.

When you sit, please don't move. Don't wiggle your toes; don't twitch or itch; don't rub; don't scratch; don't rock back and forth. Don't change your posture at all. Sit as still as the monk below. When you sit still the mind calms down. If there is any movement at all the mind will be distracted — just as Jell-O sets up, it must be cooled and not jiggled around to solidify.

Smiling

This is a smiling meditation. The reason that you should smile is that it has been found that when the corners of your mouth go up, so does your mental state. When the corners of your mouth go down, so does your mental state.[9]

Put a little smile on your lips, but do not stop there. Put a smile in your eyes even though your eyes are closed. You'll notice there can be a lot of tension in the eyes. Put a smile in your mind. And, especially, put a smile in your heart.

It can be a mechanical smile at first—eventually, it will turn into a sincere happy feeling. It should be a smile that conveys Lovingkindness. It's important to believe it! Smile with your lips, smile from your mind, and smile from your heart!

If your mind wanders away twenty-five times in a sitting, and twenty-five times you recognize it, release it, relax, re-smile, and return to your meditation, then you've had a good meditation. It definitely might not be a quiet and calm meditation, but it *is* an *active* meditation, and that can still be a *good* meditation!

Every time your mind wanders away and comes back, and you relax and smile, you are developing your ability to see a distraction and let it go. You are improving your Mindfulness, your observation power. As you practice, you will get better at it, and your powers of observation will get stronger.

---

9   Eric Jaffe, "Psychology of Smiling," *Observer* 23, no. 10 (University of Minnesota, December, 2010),
      http://www.psychologicalscience.org/index.php/publications/observer/2010/dece
      mber-10/the-psychological-study-of-smiling.html.

Distractions

While you practice Mettā meditation in this way, your mind is going to wander. What do we mean by wander? You are with your object of meditation, which is the warm glowing feeling in the center of your chest. You are experiencing this feeling; then you are distracted by some thought or sensation. It might be a sensation of itching, a desire to cough, a burning sensation, or a painful feeling in your leg. It might be a memory of a conversation with a friend or of a trip to the lake. Or it could be a thought about something you need from the store.

Suddenly you are with that distraction rather than with your object of meditation. In other words, your attention is somewhere else. You are not sure how you got there or what you are supposed to be doing. Then you *remember* that you are meditating and that you are supposed to be on your object of meditation. *Remember*— that is the first part of the definition of mindfulness.

If you let go of your thinking about the distraction and relax slightly, you can observe that there is a tight mental fist wrapped around that sensation or thought. You can also observe that you don't want it there. You want it to go away. But, the more you want it to go away, the bigger and more intense the distraction becomes.

So, your mind is on this itch, this pain, this thought. How did it get there? It didn't just jump there. There is a process that happens, and you begin to see how your mind moves from one thing to another. Don't *think* about that, but *observe* carefully how the process happens. We aren't talking here about analyzing why anything happens—simply *observe* what is happening. *Observe* the way the *mind moves and reacts* in the present—that is the second part of mindfulness.

The truth is that when a sensation is there, it's there! It's okay for it to be there. You are going to have distracting thoughts and sensations come up, and that's okay. Thoughts are not your enemy. In fact, they are opportunities.

Every thought, every feeling, every sensation that arises and distracts your mind also causes tightness.

The First Noble Truth is that there is suffering. The Second Noble Truth is that suffering is caused by Craving. The Third Noble Truth is that there is the cessation of suffering. The Fourth Noble Truth is that there is the path to the cessation of suffering. This path is the Eightfold Path.

This tightness is how you can recognize the very start of Craving and, as you may know, the Second Noble Truth says that craving is the cause of suffering! Life is not suffering; craving is what makes it so.

Distractions are telling you what you crave—the things to which you are attached. Seeing and understanding what you like and dislike is the first step toward letting go of those attachments.

Your brain has two lobes that are contained in three membranes called the *meninges*. It is like a bag wrapped around your brain and spine. Any time that there is a distraction, there is a perceptible movement in the brain, and the brain *seems* (some will disagree with this, but something is felt) to start to expand against this membrane. The thought causes tightness or tension to arise, which we can observe for ourselves.

Any time you notice this tension and tightness, you will want to actively relax this tightness and soften into it. By relaxing, you are releasing the Craving. More on this when we get to the 6Rs.

When Craving is released, there is a slight feeling of expansion in your head. Right after you relax, you will notice that your mind is very peaceful and calm. Your mind is alert, and there are no thoughts. At this time, you have a pure mind. Now bring that pure mind back to your object of meditation—the feeling of Lovingkindness and smiling—that warm, radiating, happy feeling.

Now make another wish for your happiness, put that feeling into your heart, and radiate that happy feeling to yourself.

It does not matter how many times your attention is pulled away by a distraction. Thoughts and sensations don't go away the first time you notice them, and that's okay. As these distractions come back again and again, you will become increasingly familiar with how they arise. With practice, their intensity and frequency will subside.

Hindrances

The Buddha talked about five hindrances to meditation. Hindrances are distractions that will pull you away from your object of meditation—five troublemakers who will surely come calling!

Every distraction is based on at least one of the five hindrances. Often, they come two or three at a time and gang up.

The Five Hindrances are:

1. Sensual Desire: "I like that," otherwise known as Lustful or Greedy Mind. You will hang onto things that are *pleasant* and want more. This will cause attachment to pleasant states of mind that have arisen in the past, and desire for pleasant states to arise in the future.

2. Anger, Aversion, Fear: "I don't like that." You will want to push away states of mind that you don't like. Or, you might experience fear or anger over *unpleasant* or painful feelings that have already arisen. You will try to push away and *control* anything causing you pain. You will even try to force your mind to experience things in a certain way that you think is *right* when you should just observe what is there. Now, that is really overly controlling!

3. Sloth and Torpor: Dullness and Sleepiness. These will cause lack of effort and determination because you have lost interest in your object of meditation. You will experience a mental fog. When you look at it closely, you see that it has tightness and tension in it. There is even Craving in sleepiness.

4. Restlessness: With Restlessness, you constantly want to move and change, to do something other than what you are doing, to be somewhere other than here. Restlessness can manifest as very tight, unpleasant feelings in the body and mind.

5. Doubt: You are not sure you are following the instructions correctly, or even if this is the right practice. It makes you feel unsure of yourself and may even manifest as a lack of confidence in the Buddha's teaching or your teacher or both.

When the hindrances arise, your job is neither to like them nor to fight with them. Your job is to accept them, to *invite them in*, and to "*offer them tea*"!

Don't feed them with your attention. Forcing and not liking their being there just gives them the attention they crave and makes them stronger.

That's what happens with one-pointed concentration meditation. You force the hindrances away by practicing intense concentration. However, as soon as you stop meditating they come back, sometimes even stronger.

If you just let hindrances be there, turning your attention to something that is wholesome instead, the energy inherent in them will gradually fade away. They will disappear like a fire that runs out of fuel. That's how you overcome the hindrances for good. The fire just goes out. In Pāli, Nibbāna translates as "*Ni*" or *no*, and "*bāna*" or *fire*. No Fire. No Craving. No hindrance.

The 6Rs

Now we are going to give you specific instructions on how to work with the hindrances in the way the Buddha taught.

Imagine, for a moment, the Bodhisattva resting under the Rose Apple tree as a young boy. He was not serious or tense; he was having fun, watching his father's festival. Right then he "attained to a pleasant abiding" (*jhāna*) as stated in the suttas. With a light mind, he could come to a very tranquil and aware state.

Later, on the eve of his enlightenment, after he had tried every method of meditation and bodily exercise that was known in India at that time, he remembered this state.[10] And he realized that this simple state—this tranquil, aware, and happy state—was the key to attaining awakening. But how to convey this?

When he was teaching, the Buddha worked largely with uneducated farmers and merchants. He had to have a simple, effective practice that was easy and worked quickly. He had to have a method by which everyone could experience the path and benefits for themselves easily and immediately. This is how he was able to affect so many people during his lifetime.

Do you want to see clearly? It's easy! Lighten up, have fun exploring, relax, and smile! Relaxing and smiling leads you to a happier, more interesting practice.

That sounds like great advice, but how do you do it? When you have been carried away by a distraction, and you lose your smile, just follow these steps:

1. *Recognize* that mind's attention has drifted away, and that you are lost in thought. You have forgotten what you were doing. You are no longer on your object of meditation.

---

10 Refer to Majjhima Nikāya, sutta 36:30.

2. *Release* your attachment to the thought or sensation by letting the distraction be—by not giving it any more attention. Just stop feeding it. Just back away from it.

3. *Relax* any remaining tension or tightness caused by that distraction.

4. *Re-smile.* Put that smile back on your lips and in your heart. Feel again that happy feeling of Lovingkindness.

5. *Return* or redirect. Gently redirect mind's attention back to the object of meditation, that is, to Mettā. Continue with a gentle, collected mind to stay with your object of meditation.

6. *Repeat* this entire practice cycle. Repeat this practice whenever your attention is distracted away from your object of meditation.

We call these the "6Rs." They are drawn directly from the sutta text as part of Right Effort. The first four 'R's are the four right efforts, with the last two 'R's to remind you to Return and Repeat as needed.

Notice that you never *push* anything away. You never try to control anything—trying to control is using Craving to eliminate Craving!

Please don't do the 6Rs for some slight noise in the background or a minor bodily feeling. As long as you are still with your feeling of Lovingkindness, just stay with that feeling and let it deepen. Ignore those slight distractions in the background. As a beginner do the 6Rs only if your attention is completely "gone" from the object.

In the explanation of the Eightfold Path in the suttas, one of the components is Right Effort. Right Effort and the 6Rs are the same things.

What is Right Effort?

1. You notice that an unwholesome state has arisen.

2. You stop paying attention to that unwholesome feeling, letting it be there by itself with no pushing away or holding on to it.

3. You bring up a wholesome feeling.
4. You stay with that wholesome feeling.

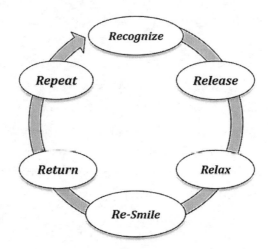

The 6Rs just add the *Return* and *Repeat* to complete the cycle. We are practicing Right Effort by repeating the 6Rs cycle again and again. We see and experience for ourselves what suffering is and how to relieve it.

You notice what causes you to become tense and tight, and then how to reach its cessation by releasing and relaxing and bringing up a wholesome object. You discover how to exercise the direct path to the cessation of suffering. This happens each time you *Recognize* and *Release* an arising feeling, *Relax,* and *Re-smile.* Notice the Relief.

When you look at the benefits discussed in the sutta about the Dhamma, there is a phrase that says the Dhamma is "*immediately effective.*" By practicing the 6Rs, you fulfill this statement! When you relax the tension or tightness caused by a distraction, you immediately experience the Third Noble Truth, the *cessation* of suffering.

In other words, you are purifying the mind by relaxing and letting go of suffering. You see this for yourself.

Then you bring up a wholesome object by *smiling*, and return mind's attention back to Mettā, which is a wholesome feeling.

You do not have to practice for long periods—months or years—to feel relief. You can see it right after the Relax step of the 6Rs. You notice the moment of a pure mind, free from Craving.

By repeating the 6Rs over and over, depriving the hindrances of attention, their fuel, you will eventually replace all of the unwholesome mental habits with wholesome ones. In this way, you bring up only wholesome states and will eventually achieve the cessation of suffering.

To be successful in meditation, you need to develop your mindfulness skill and observation power. Also, keeping up your sense of fun and exploration is important. This helps to improve your mindfulness. The 6Rs training develops these necessary skills.

Sometimes people say this practice is simpler than they thought. Some have actually complained to the teacher because they want this meditation to be more complicated!

Now let us go through each of the steps in more depth.

Recognize

Mindfulness remembers to observe and recognize movements of mind's attention from one thing to another—that is, from the meditation object to the distraction. This observing notices any movement of mind's attention away from the object of meditation. One can notice a slight tightness or tension as mind's attention begins to move toward the arising phenomenon.

Pleasant or painful feelings can occur at any one of the six sense doors. Any sight, sound, odor, taste, touch, or thought can cause a distraction to arise. With careful nonjudgmental observation, you will notice a slight tightening sensation arising both in mind and physically in the brain itself.

Recognizing early movement of mind is vital to successful meditation. You then continue on to...

Release
When a thought about something arises, release it. Let it be there without giving any more attention to it. The content of the distraction is not important at all, but the mechanics of *how* it arose are important! Don't analyze it or try to figure out why it is there; let it be without keeping mind's attention on it. Without your mind's attention, the distraction loses energy and passes away. When you do not keep your attention on it, a distraction and the mental chatter about it ceases. Mindfulness then reminds the meditator to...

Relax
After releasing the thought and allowing it to be by itself without trying to watch it or get involved in it, there is a subtle, barely noticeable tightness or tension remaining within mind and body.

To remove this remaining tension, the Buddha introduced a *relax* step. The suttas[11] call the relax step "*tranquilizing* the bodily formation." This is true especially for your head, which is part of your body.

It means to "unclench" your attention from and around the thought. It is more than just letting it go. It actively softens and relaxes, and lets the distraction be there, which then weakens its power. Gradually it disappears completely on its own.

Please do not skip this step! It is the *most important* part of this meditation. It is the *missing step* we talked about in the introduction. It is the key to progress!

---

11   This Relax step is found in all suttas where the Buddha gives meditation instructions. The Pāli word for tranquilize is *passambhaya*. See for example the Majjhima Nikāya, suttas 10:5 or 118.

Without performing this step of relaxing every time you are distracted from your meditation object, you will not experience the close-up view of the cessation of the tightness caused by Craving. You will not feel the relief as this tension is relaxed.

Remember that Craving always manifests first as a tightness or tension in both your mind and body. The *Relax* step gives you a kind of "Mundane Nibbāna." You have a momentary opportunity to see and experience the true nature of and relief from tightness and suffering while performing the *Release* and *Relax* steps. Mindfulness then continues to remember to...

Re-Smile

If you have listened to the Dhamma talks on our website, you might remember hearing about how smiling is an important aspect of the meditation. Learning to smile and raising slightly the corners of the mouth helps the mind to be observant, alert, agile, and bright. Getting serious, tensing up, or frowning causes mind to become heavy and your mindfulness to become dull and slow. Insights become more difficult to see, thus slowing down your understanding of Dhamma.

Return

Redirect your mind back to your object of meditation. Gently redirect the mind and don't "jerk" it back before you are ready. Make this a harmonious movement, a movement that is timely and not forced.

Repeat

Repeat this entire practice cycle as often as needed. Stay with your object until you slip, and then run the 6Rs again.

Spiritual Friend

For the first ten minutes of your sitting, radiate Lovingkindness to yourself. Wrap yourself up in that happy, tranquil feeling using the previous instructions. For the rest of the sitting, radiate loving and kind thoughts to a Spiritual Friend. What is a Spiritual Friend?

Now we will select our next object of meditation, the Spiritual Friend. It is very important that they are a living person, of the same sex, and are not a member of your family.

When the Spiritual Friend is of a different sex, it may lead to lustful feeling, and this complicates your experience. This is the traditional way of teaching Mettā. If this instruction does not fit you, then just make sure the person you select does not raise lustful feelings in your mind when you are radiating loving-kindness—remember, you will be spending a long time with this person.

Your Spiritual Friend should be someone who you deeply respect and sincerely wish well. They are someone who makes you smile when you think of them. It might be a favorite teacher or counselor who has your highest goals in mind. It might be a friend who always has your back and supports whatever you do.

Please do not use a member of your family as your Spiritual Friend, because family members are too close to you. Family members will be brought into your practice at a later time, but for now, they may raise hidden issues that interfere with the practice. Initially, we want to keep this easy and uncomplicated. Do not radiate to a person who is dead—the feeling will not arise correctly, as there is no personal connection that can be made.

You make the wish for your spiritual friend in this way: "As I feel this happiness in myself, may you be happy and peaceful!" Wrap them up in the feeling of Lovingkindness, place them in the center of your heart, and smile at them as you are doing this. Really be *sincere* about this; really believe it. The more you believe it, the stronger the feeling will become.

And your Friend *will* feel this. People who have been picked as spiritual friends report having these warm feelings arising in their bodies at the time you radiate mettā to them. If you ask them they will tell you they had a great week!

Continue wishing them well and see them in your mind's eye, but don't put too much emphasis on the actual mental image of them. Again, some people are very good at visualizing, and some are not. Just know who they are and that you wish them well.

The phrases are a way of priming the pump—they evoke the feeling. As you make that wish, shift your attention to the feeling itself. Remember that your object of meditation is the *feeling*. Stay with that feeling and let it grow as it will. Don't force it; just give it some gentle encouragement.

Sooner or later the feeling will fade. When it does, repeat the phrases again. It is not helpful to repeat phrases rapidly. That makes the phrase feel mechanical. Rather, say it sincerely and rest for a few moments with the feeling it evokes. Repeat a phrase again only if it hasn't brought up the feeling.

Some people ask, "Are we 'sending' or 'pushing' this feeling *outward* to the Friend?" No, we are not trying to push anything out. We are just seeing our Friend in the center of our heart and wishing for him or her to be happy. We are not sending, telegraphing, or "overnighting" any sort of feeling. When a candle radiates warmth and light, is it actively sending that feeling out? No, it radiates out because that is the nature of warmth and light. In the same way, we surround and immerse our Friend with this feeling, wishing it for them, and seeing them smiling and happy.

This process is a combination of three things arising: the radiating feeling in your heart, the mental phrase, and your image of yourself or your spiritual friend. About 75 percent of your attention should be on the radiating of the feeling, 20 percent on feeling the wish, and just a little, say 5 percent, on visualizing your spiritual friend.

Some people think they should make the visualization a bigger part of their practice. Then they complain about having tightness in their head. This is because they are pushing the idea of seeing their Spiritual Friend too much. The teacher will tell them to stop trying so hard because the most important part of Mettā is feeling the radiating—making a sincere wish for their Spiritual Friend's happiness and then feeling that happiness—not visualizing their friend.

If you are getting a headache or feeling pressure, you are *trying too hard.* Smile again and back off a little.

When you picture your spiritual friend, see them smiling and happy. Remember to keep a little smile on your lips for the entire meditation session. If you find yourself not smiling, then this will be a reminder to smile once again. Bring up another wish and send a kind feeling to your friend. Your face isn't used to smiling, so please be patient! Your cheeks might even hurt a little, but you will get used to it, and that uneasiness will pass.

Please don't criticize yourself for forgetting to smile. Critical thoughts about anything are unwholesome and lead to more suffering. This is called *judgement* thoughts. They are basically bringing aversion against yourself. It is a kind of mild self-hatred and criticism. If you see that you are coming down on yourself for forgetting to smile, then laugh with yourself for having such a crazy mind! Relax and let go of those thoughts.

Understand that everyone has a crazy mind and that it is okay to have this craziness. Laugh with yourself about it. This meditation is supposed to be fun, remember? Smile and laugh at getting caught again, then start all over with your object of meditation.

Life is a game to play, so keep everything light and have fun all of the time. It does take practice, but this is why you are doing this practice. Play with things and don't take them too seriously.

This is a serious meditation, but we do not want you to *be serious!* Your mind should not be too serious; rather, it should be light and uplifted. Smile, and if that does not work, then laughing a little bit should help you get back into that happier, alert state of mind.

You will use the same Spiritual Friend the entire time until the teacher says you can change. This may be a few days or weeks. If practicing on your own, get in touch with us via the website and let us help you. You can become part of our Yahoo discussion group). The more you can stay in the present—happy and content, feeling happiness with your Spiritual Friend—the sooner you will be able to move on to the next step of the meditation. You can always contact us through our website for guidance.

Once you have settled on a good Spiritual Friend, stay with that person. If you switch from one person to another, the practice won't be able to ripen or deepen. Sometimes meditators want to send Mettā to other people, or to all beings. This is just a subtle way your mind distracts you. You want to stay with the same friend in the beginning so that you can build your *collectedness.*

We replace the word "concentration" with the word *collectedness* to help clarify that we are not forcing our minds to stay on only one object of meditation in a forceful, fixed way. Rather, we want our mind to rest lightly on the object. If your mind wanders, use the 6Rs.

When there are no distractions, there is no need to exert any effort to keep your mind on its object. It just stays there by itself.

That is really an amazing thing to see happen!

Again, there may be times that some random thoughts and sensations arise while you are on your object of meditation but which are not strong enough to pull your attention away completely from it. When this happens, ignore those and stay with your meditation object. These thoughts and distractions will go away by themselves; there is no need to 6R them.

So, let's review:

1. Sit for a minimum of thirty minutes (why is explained later).
2. *Begin* by radiating kind and happy thoughts and wishes to yourself for about *ten* minutes.
3. *Switch* to your one chosen Spiritual Friend for the remainder of your sitting—at least *twenty minutes*—and radiate kind and happy thoughts to them for the rest of the session. Stay with just the same Friend and do not switch to anything or anyone else, even if you think they "deserve" your attention. Such desires are just more distractions. The mind can be very sneaky!
4. *Use the 6Rs* to overcome distractions.

When the feeling of Mettā starts to become stronger, notice it and sink into it — smile into it and let it develop by itself. If you find that you are subtly verbalizing the phrases and the verbalizing starts to cause some tightness, let go of the verbalization and just feel the wish. This will allow the feeling to grow even stronger. Stay with the feeling and just be in the moment without pushing or "leaning into" it.

This practice will take time to master. In a sense, this is a kind of "not-doing"—you are not controlling or pushing the feeling, you are just gently directing it. If there is tension in your body from trying to send it out, then you are putting in too much effort. There should just be the wish for happiness, in the same way, you wish someone good luck on a journey. You stand and wave as they go—you don't stand and try to push a feeling out to them! Similarly, with Mettā meditation, you simply smile and wish this feeling of gentle Lovingkindness.

After doing the 6Rs and getting the hang of it, there will be a hindrance that arises. Finally, you 6R the last little bit of tension from it, and it disappears completely! Craving is eliminated for the first time. A small amount of craving is gone, never to arise again.

Because of the hindrance disappearing Joy arises and, for the first time, you are experiencing the first *Tranquil Aware Jhāna*. There will be more to go as you progress along this path. As your practice advances, you will find that the joy is there. It can be goose bumps, thrills, or just excitement arising. A pleasant, tranquil feeling will follow it.

As you go deeper, your confidence gets stronger, and you understand that what you are doing is right practice. Also, you will notice there is a much deeper state of quiet in your mind than you have ever experienced before. It is like someone turned off the refrigerator you never even realized was on.

You might notice that you are not aware of parts of your body unless you direct your attention to them. This is a normal development as your body starts to lose tension and tightness, and this indicates progress.

Finally, as you get deeper, the feeling of Lovingkindness may rise into your head. Never try to control the feeling—if it wants to move there, then let it move.

Now you have become an advanced meditator.

When this happens, you will be ready for the next step of the meditation practice. Contact us through our website. We will not cover that here, as this is now advanced practice and requires more instructions. You are now on your way through the Tranquil Aware Jhānas to the experience of awakening.

Forgiveness Meditation

There may be for some difficulty with bringing up and sustaining the feeling of loving-kindness — even after following all the instructions and guidance here. You may bring up a phrase, "May I be happy, may I be content" and this causes self-aversion or hatred to arise. "I don't deserve it, I am not a nice person," may arise in your mind. You try the 6R's, and it doesn't really work. There is no loving-kindness there, your heart just has no feeling and is dry and maybe hard.

You may find the practice of Forgiveness Meditation will help with this. We find now a not so small percentage of students benefit tremendously from switching to Forgiveness in which you radiate forgiveness to yourself and forgiving everything that comes up and as people come up, you forgive them until they forgive you.

You can find out more about this practice at the Dhamma Sukha website and in a book called *Forgiveness Meditation* by Bhante Vimalaraṁsi. This small forgiveness book, as well as the text of this book, has also been included as an appendix in the more complete book about this practice, *The Path to Nibbana* by David Johnson.

Forgiveness is about letting go of the past and softening our minds. Everyone can benefit from practicing forgiveness.

Walking Meditation

An important part of the Mettā practice is Walking Meditation. Please do not ignore it. You need to walk to keep your energy up, especially after longer sittings.

You can use Walking Meditation to build energy or uplift your mind before sitting if you feel sleepy or have low energy.

Sometimes, when your mind is distracted, walking will make it easier to calm a restless mind so that you can go back to sitting. Walking Meditation, on the other hand, can add energy to your sitting by getting your blood flowing.

Walking Meditation is a powerful meditation on its own but, in conjunction with Mettā Meditation, it helps you to incorporate Mettā into your everyday life and activities. Please do remember that this is an all-the-time practice.

Find a place to walk that is at least thirty paces and is straight and level. Walk at a normal pace as if you are taking a stroll in the park on a Sunday afternoon; not slowly like a turtle, but at a speed that is neither too fast nor too slow. Your eyes should be directed down in front of you six to ten feet ahead.

Do not put your attention on your feet. Instead, stay with your Spiritual Friend. Please do not look around, as that will distract you from your meditation. This is not a nature walk, but part of the actual practice where you are radiating kind and happy thoughts to your Spiritual Friend. As much as possible, stay with that practice the entire time you are walking. It is just like when you are sitting, with the only difference being that you are walking instead of sitting.

You may do this inside or outside as the weather permits. It is best done outside in the open air, but try to avoid the heat of direct sunlight. You can also walk inside, in a circular path around a room or down a hallway.

Some meditators make a lot of progress while walking — it can go quite deep. Do not take this instruction lightly as it is an important part of the practice. It also helps us learn how to practice Mettā in our everyday life where we are more active out in the world.

Walk for about fifteen to thirty minutes and never more than an hour, as this much walking will tire your body out. However, do walk at a good pace so that by the end of it, you will feel your heart pumping and you may be slightly out of breath. Then you can sit and be fully alert. Walking can bring calmness, clarity, *or* energy, depending on what you need at the time.

Keep it Going

Thirty minutes of meditation a day is the minimum to start. From our experience, it takes fifteen to twenty minutes to get the mind to settle down. Then you are giving yourself another ten productive minutes where you can truly watch and observe. Forty-five minutes is better.

Just the fact you are sitting and not moving permits the mind to calm down. The longer you sit the more your mind will calm on its own, without you doing anything else. So, sitting longer and not moving is vital to progress to deeper states.

On retreat, you will at first sit at least thirty minutes, walk fifteen minutes, then sit again, alternating like this for the whole day. Your sittings will naturally get longer and longer throughout the retreat and may eventually last as long as two to three hours.

In your daily life, sitting twice a day is very helpful. Once you are comfortable, try to stay completely still throughout the sitting period. If the mind insists on moving, 6R the desire to move. The 6Rs are very helpful in dissolving tension and finding deeper ease.

If pain arises, please watch *how* it arises. You can tell if the pain is genuine by noticing what happens when you get up from sitting. If the pain goes away very quickly, it is a "meditation pain," which is, in fact, a mental pain and is not caused by anything harmful. It is just a distraction. If it returns when you sit, try to remain still and 6R. If, when you get up, the pain lingers and stays with you, it is best not to sit that way in the future, because this would be actual physical pain manifesting.

If we try to get rid of painful or unpleasant feelings forcefully, whether mental or physical, we just add more greed and aversion to the mind. This fuels the vicious cycle of *Saṃsāra*. However, if we approach an unpleasant feeling openly and without taking it personally, we view these unwholesome qualities with *wholesome* awareness. This pure, clear awareness gradually melts that disturbing feeling. Moreover, you might notice the feeling linger, but your attitude toward it has changed.

If you get sleepy sitting inside, try sitting outside but not in the direct sun. The outdoors tends to wake you up. You can even try doing the walking practice backward after you walk forward thirty paces. Instead of turning around, just walk backward to the starting point.

Meditation and its benefits increase if you can continue to cultivate awareness throughout the day. Smile and send Mettā whenever you think of it. When you notice difficult feelings coming up, 6R them. Do this with a sense of fun and humor at just how crazy mind can be. If you get serious and try to control the mind, that is just more Craving. You may wear yourself out and become frustrated. So do this lightly, but with as much continuity as possible.

Add Mettā to Everything

You can bring Lovingkindness into everything that you do. Generally, you will do your sitting at home, but you can also smile and radiate well-being and happiness to all beings when you are out and about. If you are just going out walking or shopping, you do not have to stay with a Spiritual Friend. Stay with a general feeling of Mettā.

Smile more. Notice and 6R emotional upsets that arise. When unwholesome states of mind arise, see them as opportunities. Let them be and bring up wholesome ones. This is the meaning of Right Effort in the Buddha's Noble Eightfold Path.

Progress and Jhāna

As you make progress with the meditation, you will see all kinds of new phenomena. Joy and other pleasant experiences will arise. Some of them will be really worth the price of admission!

The first time you truly and completely let go of a hindrance, you will have your first experience of the jhānic state and be on your way to going even deeper. You will start to be friends with fun stuff like Joy, Contentment, Equanimity, and more. Good times are on the way!

Brahmavihāras and Nibbāna

The Buddha talked about four divine qualities of mind that are particularly wholesome. They are called the *Brahmavihāras* and consist of Lovingkindness (*Mettā*), Compassion (*karuṇā*), Sympathetic Joy (*muditā*)–we actually prefer just Joy–and Equanimity (*upekkhā*). This is the practice you are starting now. You will gradually go through all these states very naturally as Mettā becomes quieter and turns to compassion and so on through joy to equanimity. You do not need to change the practice as you go–the states themselves will develop and arise on their own.

Once you become an advanced meditator, you just have to keep the meditation going. The Brahmavihāras develop naturally, one by one, without you having to bring up each of these states as its own separate meditation object. When the next state arises, then you take that state, whether it be compassion or joy as the feeling, to be the object of meditation and continue radiating that out now.

This is another important difference from how other practices have you develop Mettā. The Buddha taught that when the meditation is properly practiced, all four divine states arise on their own one after the other.[12] You will learn how to radiate any of these four states to all the six directions and then to all directions at the same time.

As this happens, the *jhānas* will arise naturally on their own as well. The word jhāna is a loaded word. It has been translated in many different ways, but we refer to the jhānas as levels of understanding. We do not want to confuse them with their one-pointed absorption jhāna cousins. They are related, but these are ones in which the meditator keeps awareness of their body, whereas the others do not. The Buddha taught that the key to understanding

---

12   Majjhima Nikāya, sutta 43:31, shows the progression of radiating into all directions starting with Lovingkindness.

Craving and distractions is to realize that mind *and* body are one process that cannot be separated. Tension and tightness are bodily processes, while thought and images are mental processes. We not only want to pay attention to the mind but also be aware of what is happening in the body and not ignore or repress this awareness through one-pointed focused concentration.

We call the jhānic states that we experience with this meditation the *Tranquil Aware Jhānas*. There are eight of them (four *rūpa* or "material" jhānas, and four *arūpa* or "immaterial" jhānas). Beyond the highest immaterial jhāna lies the experience of Nibbāna itself. Your mind will become so quiet that it just stops. When the mind comes back from that cessation experience, it will be incredibly bright and clear, with no disturbance—like a blackboard with nothing on it.

At that point, when the next mental process arises, you will see with astonishing clarity every link and part of this process that we call life as it arises and passes away. This process is what the Buddha called Dependent Origination. There are twelve links in each moment of experience, and you will see how all of these arise and pass away. You will see how all of these dependently arise one upon the other.

When you see very deeply into this process, you will understand, on a profound personal level, that all of the "aggregates" that make up "you," or the "I," are impersonal and without any enduring self or soul. This experience is so profound that Nibbāna will arise, and you will understand the true nature of all existence. You will have attained awakening in this very life — there will be so much relief!

Experiencing awakening (Nibbāna) happens for many people who follow these simple directions. It does not take years or decades. The Buddha said that this practice is "immediately effective." In the Satipaṭṭhāna Sutta of the Majjhima Nikāya, he says that this experience can take place in as little as seven years, or even seven days. It can truly happen that fast; we have seen it take place within a single eight-day retreat. So, start now, and you too can experience the initial stages of awakening. Just follow the instructions exactly!

Benefits of Lovingkindness

There are many benefits to practicing Lovingkindness meditation. In the suttas, it says that when you practice Mettā meditation, you go to sleep easily and sleep soundly. You have no nightmares. When you wake up, you awaken easily and quickly. People really like you! Animals like you. Your face becomes radiant and beautiful. You have good health. These are just a few of the benefits.

When you practice Lovingkindness, your mind also becomes clear and quiet, and your progress in the meditation is very fast.

Mettā in Daily Life

Continue to sit and practice. Listen to talks, read our books, and study more about the concepts surrounding this practice. There are many resources on our website.

When starting any new practice, it is usually best to immerse yourself in that practice, setting aside other practices you may have done in the past, until you understand the new practice deeply and thoroughly. Otherwise, you may be confused with the various opinions and practices that are out there.

Remember that we are not basing our teaching on views or opinions, but rather on the study of the suttas themselves and the direct experience of the meditation practice. We invite you to follow this path as well.

The best way to experience deep immersion into Tranquil Wisdom Insight Meditation is to come for a retreat or if you cannot get away, do an online retreat with us. Check our website for more information.

Once you master staying with the Spiritual Friend, there are more instructions for breaking down barriers and radiating the feeling of Mettā in all directions. The teacher will give you those directions and advise you when you are ready. This is where the practice of the Brahmavihāras really takes off.

More phenomena will arise, and a teacher can guide you based on your progress. There are more instruction steps in this practice, but they are advanced. A new book is available that covers these advanced instructions and all the advanced jhānas up to and including the experience of Nibbāna — *The Path to Nibbāna* by David Johnson — available everywhere in paper or eBook.

For now, master the ability to stay with your Spiritual Friend perfectly, and then you could contact us for further advice, do a retreat, or buy the advanced book noted above and practice on your own.

Again, when you are outside moving around in daily life, remember to smile and radiate Mettā to all beings. Use Right Effort to recondition your mind. Bring up the wholesome quality of Lovingkindness instead of allowing whatever "ho-hum" mind is there.

Stuck in a long line at the checkout line? Radiate Mettā. It is a tough job being a cashier at a store, so smile at the cashier and be friendly.

Traffic bogged down, and you just can't move? Rather than getting upset, radiate Mettā to your fellow drivers. 6R your upset mind and replace it with a wholesome, uplifted mind. Put a CD in the car player and listen to a Dhamma talk to learn more about the Eightfold Path of the Buddha, rather than wasting your own time ho-humming your way through life.

Share what you have learned with other people, and let them benefit from your practice. Pay this practice forward once you understand it. Don't proselytize! Just talk about what happened to you in your own words. How is it helping you be happier? Be *the Buddha* rather than a *Buddhist!*

Can't find a sitting group in your area? Start your own. As soon as you find one more person, you have a group! Meditate for at least thirty minutes, listen to a talk, have some tea and discuss what you have learned. Right there, you have just created your own sitting group!

Little by little, like drops of water filling a cup, you will soon come to supreme awakening. It is possible to do this right now. The Buddha showed us the way. Just follow the instructions *exactly*!

Now go sit!

Resources

Dhamma Sukha Meditation Center website:
http://www.dhammasukha.org

Books

Kraft, Doug. *Buddha's Map: His Original Teachings on Awakening, Ease, and Insight in the Heart of Meditation.* Grass Valley, CA: Blue Dolphin Publishing, 2013.

Vimalaraṁsi, Bhante. *Breath of Love.* Jakarta, Indonesia: Ehipassiko Foundation of Indonesia, 2012.

———. *Meditation Is Life; Life Is Meditation.* Annapolis: Dhamma Sukha Publishing, 2014.

———. *Moving Dhamma,* Vol. 1. Annapolis: Dhamma Sukha Publishing, 2012.

Johnson, David. *The Path to Nibbāna.* Annapolis, Dhamma Sukha Publishing, 2017

Contact
Dhamma Sukha Meditation Center
8218 County Road 204
Annapolis, MO 63620
info@dhammasukha.org

Acknowledgements

This book was written with and edited by David Johnson, who added content accumulated and compiled from our many meditation students' experiences. Additional editing by Teri Pohl, Jens Tröger, founder of Bookalope and Danielle Loesch.

Also, we wish to acknowledge Bhikkhu Bodhi for his excellent translations of the Majjhima Nikāya and the Saṃyutta Nikāya, and for his past support. We want to credit Wisdom Publications for the sutta quotations used from Anupada Sutta, Number 111 in the Majjhima Nikāya.

Sharing Merit

May Suffering ones be suffering free

and the fear-struck, fearless be,

May the grieving shed all grief,

and may all beings find relief.

May all beings share this merit

that we have thus acquired,

for the acquisition of all kinds of happiness.

May beings inhabiting Space and Earth,

Devas and Nāgas of mighty power,

share in this merit of ours.

May they long protect the Buddha's Dispensation.

Sādhu, Sādhu, Sādhu.

70728388R00034

Made in the USA
San Bernardino, CA
06 March 2018